The Calabrian way
Food from the Heart

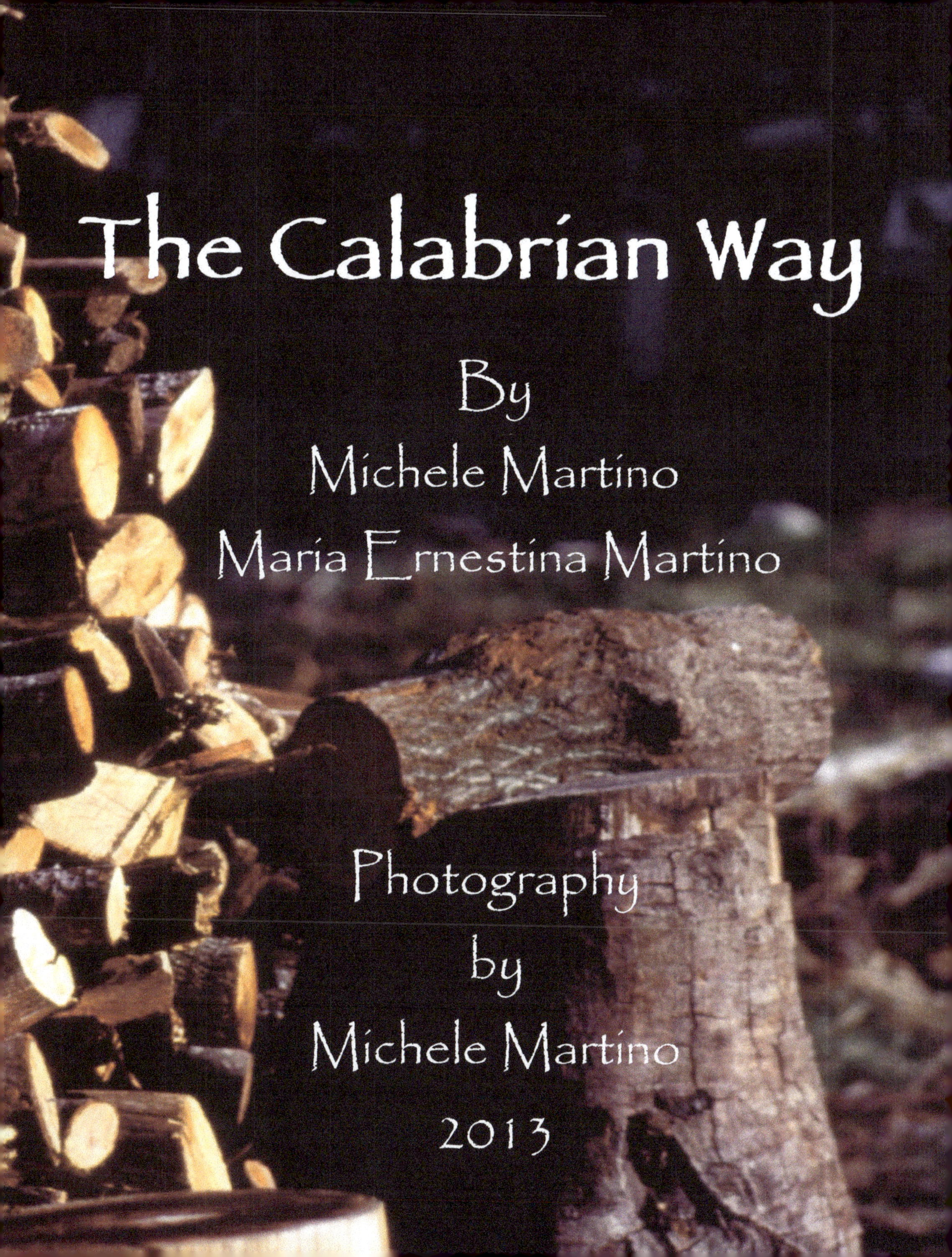

The Calabrian Way

By

Michele Martino

Maria Ernestina Martino

Photography

by

Michele Martino

2013

Contents

Baccala cu brodo di Patane	87	Olivi ammacati	23
Biscotti cu icing Sugar	169	Panini, Pitta e' Pane	181
Biscotti cu Pinozzi	167	Panzarotti	31
Biscotti di Mamma	166	Pasta al Forno Part A	59
Biscotti Lungi	165	Pasta al Forno Part B	60
Cannelloni	57	Pasta e' Ciciri	65
Canolli	163	Pasta e' Patane	63
Carna alla Pizzaiola	146	Pasta e' Pisiddri	64
Cassata	170	Pasta e' Vruoccucli	66
Cotaletti	145	Pastina	68
Crema di Zia Concetta	177	Patane e' Pipazzi	101
Crostolli	172	Pisiddri	90
Curirieddri	27	Pitticeddri di Yuri	121
Favi	103	Pitticeddri di Mulangiana	123
Ficutu e' Pipazzi	152	Pitticeddri di Patane	117
Frisa	34	Pitticeddri di Riso	115
Fritata di Cipuddra	99	Pitticeddri di Vruoccucli	119
Fritata di Pipazzi	100	Pizzette	33
Funci fritti cu Farina	35	Pollo arrustutu	151
Funci sutta olio	36	Porkbelly Vrascioli	144
Giardinieri	26	Purrpetti	147
Gnocchi	53	Purrputunu	148
Grispeddri	29	Rapi e' Savuzizza	150
Insalata di Fasuoli	104	Risotto cu Mince	91
Insalata di Pommodore	97	Savuzizza Calabrese	149
Insalata di Tonno e' Pommodore	98	Scapica	25
		Scavudatieddri	179
Insalata di Vruoccucli	93	Spaghetti cu aglia, olio e' sinisu	67
Jelly Tart di Zia Lisa	171		
Lagana e' Ciciri	61	Sucu	51
Lagana e' fasuoli	62	Tiramisu	173
Lasagna	52	Torrone	175
Lenticchie	88	Turdiddri	174
Maccaruni	55	Verdura cu Patane e' sinisu	92
Minestra di Mulangiana	124	Vrascioli	143
Minestra di Patane	89	Vruoccucli alla Tiedra	94
Minestrone	96	Yakkateddri	24
Mulangiana alla Parmigiana	122	Zuchini di Papa	95

Autumn awaits as I near my birth town in the Calabrian mountains of Southern Italy.
My hillside village of Fagnano Castello still surprises me in awe as it blends and contrasts with the surrounding chestnut forests to create a picture of peace and tranquillity.

While memories flood my senses of previous visits in years past, I wonder..... is Ciccio's bar still open for coffee or a quick pre dinner apperativo.

As I approach and wander through the narrow streets a warm rush of contentment settles my anxiousness......little has changed, my town is still with me and in me.

The four seasons bring their own individual qualities to the town and its people as daily life adapts to the changes.
The winter sun rises to reveal a blanket of snow over the rustic terracotta roofs and the air is filled with the sweet smell of smoke from warm fireplaces.

THE SONG OF CHURCH BELLS ROLL ACROSS THE HILLS AS CHRISTMAS DAY MASS ENDS AND FAMILIES GATHER FOR THEIR LONG FESTIVE LUNCH.

IN THE BARS, SHORT BLACK COFFEE AND GRAPPA ARE SUITED TO THE SHORT COLD DAYS OF WINTER.
THE BARE WINTER TREES, WILD FLOWERS AND STONE FRUITS COME TO LIFE ACROSS THE OPEN SLOPES, SIGNALING THE WARMING DAYS OF SPRING.
THE TRAVELING MARKETS HAVE ALSO RETURNED BRINGING THEIR OWN DIVERSE VIBRANT LIFE FULL OF SMELLS, SOUNDS AND COLORS.

IN THE COUNTRY FIELDS IT'S TIME TO START PLANTING EVERY IMAGINABLE VEGETABLE IN PREPARATION FOR THE FULLNESS OF DAILY LIFE IN SUMMER.

THE CAREFREE SEASON HAS ARRIVED, WHERE FOOD AND LEISURE FIND A HAPPY BALANCE.
THE WARM SUN GIVES LIFE TO RIPE RED TOMATOES, EGGPLANT, WILD FENNEL AND OTHER HAND PLANTED PLANTS WHICH WILL END UP ON THE TABLE AS FOOD.

THE LONG DAYS ARE ENJOYED WITH GELATO, COFFEE, SWEETS, A FRESH PANINI OR A LONG LINGERING ALFRESCO LUNCH UNDER A GRAPE VINE PERGOLA OR THE GREEN LEAFY SHADE OF AN OLD CHESTNUT TREE.

THE CHESTNUT LEAVES SLOWLY CHANGE TO ORANGE AND BROWN AS THE HOT SUMMER DAYS TURN TO COOL AUTUMN. YOUNG AND OLD THE FAGNANISI SCOUR THE HILLS SEARCHING FOR WILD PORCINI MUSHROOMS WHICH WILL END UP COOKED FRESH FOR LUNCH.

THE TIME HAS ALSO ARRIVED TO PICK THE GRAPES......
WITH ONE THOUGHT IN MIND .....WINE.
AS THE CHILL RETURNS IN THE AIR, A WARM FIREPLACE,
ROASTED CHESTNUTS, A BOTTLE OF HOMEMADE
RED WINE, LAUGHTER WITH FAMILY AND FRIENDS......
THIS IS THE MAGICAL LASTING MEMORY WHICH KEEPS
MY JOURNEY THROUGH LIFE ALIVE.

DELMA IMMIGRATED TO AUSTRALIA IN 1951, FOLLOWED
BY FRANCESCHINA IN 1965 AND STARTED THEIR NEW
LIVES AND FAMILIES IN AUSTRALIA, A LAND WHICH
AT THAT TIME DID NOT OFFER THE CULINARY
DELIGHTS WE ALL ENJOY TODAY.
THEY SETTLED ON THE LAND FARMING TOBACCO, AND
COOKING FOR THE FAMILY AND FARM WORKERS USING
THE PRODUCE THAT THEY GREW IN THE BACK YARD.

OVER THE YEARS, AS COOKS DO, THEY MADE SLIGHT
MODIFICATIONS TO SOME OF THE TRADITIONAL
ELEMENTS OF THEIR FOOD TO REFLECT THEIR
PERSONALITY.

GROWING UP IN THIS ENVIRONMENT, WE AS CHILDREN,
WERE TREATED TO THE MANY DELIGHTS WHICH BECAME
NORMAL FOR US BUT WHICH STILL TO THIS DAY HAVE
NOT MADE IT TO MAINSTREAM COMMERCIAL COOKING.

THE REAL JOURNEY THROUGH FAGNANO CASTELLO
BEGAN IN THE SPRING OF 1934 WHEN
DELMA POMPEA BELLOMUSTO WAS BORN
AND LATER ON IN SUMMER OF 1936, WITH
FRANCESCHINA SBARRA.

THEY, OUR MOTHERS, UN-BEKNOWN
TO EACH OTHER AS CHILDREN, PLAYED IN THE NARROW
STREETS AND COURTYARDS, PLANTED THE TOMATOES,
PICKED THE WILD STRAWBERRIES AND FENNEL AND
COOKED THE SEASONAL FOODS.

CALABRIA SHOWED THEM
THE TRUE WAY TO
NURTURE THE NATURAL
FRUITS OF THE
LAND AND HOW TO
COMBINE THEM TO CREATE
SIMPLE YET UNFORGETTABLE........

FOOD FROM THE HEART.

AS ADULTS WE SOON BEGAN TO UNDERSTAND HOW IMPORTANT IT WAS TO GET ALL THIS KNOWLEDGE ON PAPER FOR THE ENJOYMENT OF MANY GENERATIONS TO COME.

SO OUR JOURNEY BEGAN, BY GETTING OUR MOTHERS TO COOK ALL THE RECIPES AND FOR US TO WRITE THEM DOWN AND THEN TAKE PHOTOS.
THIS WAS A TASK IN ITSELF, HAVING TO SLOW THEM DOWN TO TAKE ACCURATE MEASUREMENTS OF EACH INGREDIENT AND OF COURSE THEY WERE NOT HAPPY WITH JUST MAKING ONE DISH AT A TIME ..... 3 TO 4 AT A TIME, DEPENDING ON THE COMPLEXITY OF THE RECIPES.

WE WATCHED IN AWE AS THEY WORKED THE INGREDIENTS FROM MEMORY ONTO THE PLATES, ONTO THE STOVE OR INTO THE OVEN AND FINALLY ONTO THE TABLE AS A..................................
TRUE AUTHENTIC CALABRIAN FEAST.

OUR THANKS TO ZIA ANNA LAVALLE FOR SHOWING US AND MAKING CANOLLI AND CROSTOLLI.

OUR DEAREST THOUGHTS ARE WITH THE RELATIVES WHO ARE FEATURED IN OUR BOOK BUT SADLY HAVE PASSED AWAY.

ZIO ANTONIO.................................PAGE 38

ZIO ANTONIO SBARRA..........PAGE 42

SANTUZZU...................................PAGE 44

ZIO NINUCIO..............................PAGE 141

ZIA AQUILINA.............................PAGE 189

ZIA RITA......................................PAGE 191

A FEW DISHES FOR A TYPICAL SUNDAY FEAST

Il Paese

FAGNANO CASTELLO

High in the
calabrian
mountains
the hillside village
awakens
to the
mellow glow of a
warm
autumn sunrise

INSPIRED FROM THE OLD........
THE NEW PALLAZI
MARK THEIR OWN
MOMENT IN HISTORY....
ALL EXIST AS ONE.

IN THE CENTRO STORICO WALLS ARE
ALIVE WITH TEXTURE REVEALING
THE PAST...
HARDSHIPS.. IMPROVISATIONS..
NOTHING TO HIDE......

AS YOU WANDER THE STREETS
....SMALL TREASURES APPEAR

IL PORTONE

KNOCK, YOU'RE ALWAYS WELCOME

ART. 663 C.P.
DIVIETO DI AFFISSIONE

PIAZZA
ALDO MORO

BACKYARDS......
NO PRETENSE......
ALL SERVING A PURPOSE.

La Casa

She stands tall and proud
.......void of decoration
in times gone by.....
Children are born....
Food is cooked.......
The family sleeps.....
Daughters are married....
Nonna grows old...
The home has seen it all

Olivi Ammacati

INGREDIENTS
Makes 3 packets

Start with 2 Kg of green olives.

Dressing for each packet

- 2 cloves of thinly sliced garlic
- Salt to taste
- 1 teaspoon of Paprika
- 1 teaspoon of fennel seeds
- 3 tablespoons of olive oil

Disposable gloves
(removing seeds from the olives stains your fingers so use gloves)
Remove seed by banging with an empty beer bottle
(this method seems to be the most effective)
Remove seed and place the olives in a large container full of fresh clean water. Replace water daily for 7 days
After 7 days place the olives in a large delicate laundry bag and place in the washing machine. Put the setting on the washing machine on spin and let the machine go through the spin cycle.
Place in sandwich size zip lock bags and place in the freezer.
When you want to use the olives remove bag from freezer and let them thaw at room temperature.
Once completely thawed out gently squeeze any excess moisture out of the olives. Pat dry with paper towel.

Dress with ingredients.
In a bowl place the thawed green olives.
Mix through remaining ingredients until well mixed.
Place in a jar with lid and keep in fridge.

Yakkateddri

Bring olive oil to boil the in small deep pan

Add sun dried capsicum (2-3 at a time) into boiling oil for 10 sec.
Make sure the cooked strips are crunchy.
Remove and drain off excess oil into pan

Place on a flat plate
Once all the capsicum are cooked, sprinkle with salt.

INGREDIENTS
Serves 4 persons

- Hand full of sun dried capsicum strips
- Olive oil
- 2 pinches of salt

Scapica

INGREDIENTS
Makes 1 1/2 litres

- 2kg eggplant (large to med sized)
- Salt (enough to salt eggplant)
- 1 lemon cut into quarters
- Cup of small leaf mint
- 4 large cloves of garlic thinly sliced
- 1 red capsicum thinly sliced
- 3 sticks of celery thinly sliced
- 1 3/4 litres of white vinegar
- 4 cups of water
- 2 cups of vegetable oil

Peel eggplant and cut into thin slices approx 3mm tk. Place in large bowl in layers and salt well and add lemon quarters. Cover with large plate and apply weight (10kg) for 24 hours. The next day, add vinegar and water into saucepan and bring to the boil. Rinse eggplant under water and squeeze dry by hand. Do only small handfuls at a time and place in boiling water and vinegar mixture. Stir until the eggplant turns white, (Do not over cook the eggplant this step should only take a few moments) then remove and place in colander and strain. Transfer the eggplant onto a dry cloth and spread out evenly to dry. Once eggplant is cool pat with paper towel to absorb the remaining moisture. To dress place 1 layer of dried eggplant into a container and sprinkle mint, garlic, capsicum and celery on top. Layer again with eggplant and again with mint, garlic etc. Repeat this layering until the container is almost full. Pour vegetable oil over the eggplant to cover. Place lid on container and store in fridge

Giardinieri

Boil vinegar, oil and sugar in a large deep pot
At the boil add carrots, after 3 minutes add beans
and after an extra 3 minutes add the cauliflower, zucchini, and celery
and cook for 10 minutes.
Then add the capsicum last and then cook for a further
10 minutes and stir occasionally.
All the ingredients need to end up aldente..not over cooked.
Take off the stove and drain into colander.
Reserve the liquid for later. Spread all the ingredients onto a
paper towel to dry and cool. Allow liquid to cool as well.
Place all the dry ingredients into a jar and gently press down by hand.
Pour the cooled liquid into the jar and make sure all the
ingredients are covered. Seal tight and place in fridge.
Serve cold.

INGREDIENTS
Makes a 2 Litre Jar

- 200 gms of green beans. Chop into 3 cm pieces
- 1 carrot cut into thin strips
- 300 gms of cauliflower- cut into flowerettes
- 1 zucchini cut into thin strips
- 1 stick of celery cut into small pieces
- 1 litre of white vinegar
- 3/4 cups of sugar
- 3/4 cups of olive oil

Curirieddri

INGREDIENTS
Makes approx 35 potato rings

- 1 Kg potatoes
- 1 teaspoon of salt
- 300 gms of plain flour
- ½ cup of self raising flour
- 20 gms fresh yeast
- 1/3 cup of milk
- vegetable oil to suit size of pan (500mls approx)

Boil whole potatoes in water (do not peel)
Once cooled peel cooked potatoes
Mash potatoes in large mixing bowl

In a small bowl add milk and yeast.
Dissolve the yeast by mixing it round with the milk
Add both flours to mashed potatoes mix and the yeast mixture.
Mix by hand and knead until smooth.

Cut a fist size piece of the firm mixture and roll by hand into 1 cm dia long rolls. Cut off a 25 cm piece and curl into a ring.
Press ends together with your finger to stick together.
Continue this procedure with all the potato mixture till all the rings are formed.

Bring vegetable oil to boil in large frying pan. Fill the pan enough for deep frying to cover the thickness of the potato rings.
Place potato rings (as many as can fit) into boiling oil and deep fry.
When one side is golden brown flip over and cook the other side till golden brown.
Once cooked remove and drain excess oil into pan and place
On paper towels to further drain excess oil.
Place on platter for serving.

28

Grispeddri

INGREDIENTS
Makes 30 pieces

- 1 kg of plain flour
- 1 tablespoon of fresh yeast
- Water
- Pinch of Salt
- Anchovies

In a medium sized bowl place flour, water, yeast and mix by hand. The consistency should be a bit softer than pizza dough. With both hands, grab some dough and place one anchovy in the middle, twist slightly and gently drop into boiling oil in deep frying pan.
Allow to cook until golden brown and turn over to cook the other side.
Place on absorbent paper to drain excess oil.
Place on flat dish for serving. Best eaten hot to warm.

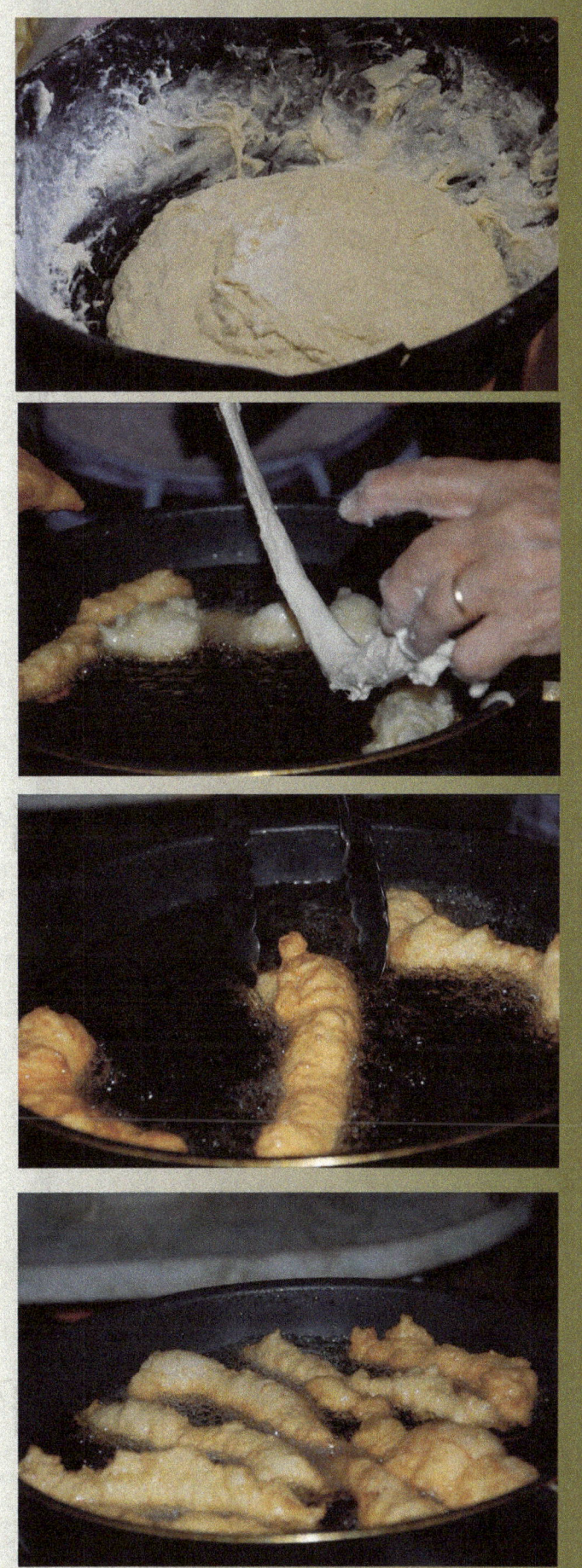

Panzarotti

INGREDIENTS
Makes approx 30 Panzzarotti

FILLING:
- 500gms mince
- 2 ripe tomatoes- pureed
- 1 crushed garlic
- 25 mls white wine
- 50gms grated mozzarella cheese
- 3 Basil leaves finely chopped

DOUGH:
- 30 grms fresh yeast
- 800 mls of water
- 1 1/2 teaspoons of salt
- 1 kg plain flour
- Vegetable oil for cooking.

Mix yeast, water and salt in a large bowl. Add flour and mix by hand to even dough consistency. Note: add water as required for correct consistency. Cover with cloth and allow to rise.

Heat oil in a saucepan. Add garlic and onions and cook until the onions are soft.
Add mince and wine and stir until browned.
Add a handful of grated mozzarella cheese and stir.
Add pureed tomatoes and basil.
Bring sauce to the boil for 1 minute and then simmer for 30 minutes

Knead dough and roll into long rolls approx 5 cm diameter.
Cut into 8 cm pieces and roll into a ball.
Before placing the mixture on the dough flatten with fingers to approx 1 1/2cm thick patty.
Re flatten again with palm of hand to approx 1cm thick patty.

Spread approx 1 tablespoon of cooked mince into centre of dough patty.
Fold each patty and press edges with fingers to close.
Heat the vegetable oil in a large frying pan till it's very hot.
Place the panzarotti in the oil and cook each side till golden brown.
Drain excess oil onto adsorbent paper.
Serve warm to hot.

Pizzetti

INGREDIENTS
Makes 30 Pizzetti

- 2 ripe tomatoes - pureed
- 1 crushed garlic
- 50gms grated mozzarella cheese
- 3 Basil leaves finely chopped
- 30 gms fresh yeast
- 800 mls of water
- 1 1/2 teaspoons of salt
- 1 kg plain flour
- 3 tablespoons of olive oil for sauce
- Vegetable oil

Mix yeast, water and salt in large bowl.
Add flour and mix by hand to even dough consistency.
Note: add water as required for correct consistency.
Cover with cloth and allow to rise.

Heat oil in pan add garlic and cook for one minute.
Add pureed tomatoes and basil.
Bring sauce to boil and then simmer for 30 minutes

Knead dough and roll into a long roll approx 5 cm diameter.
Cut into 8 cm pieces and roll into ball.
Flatten with fingers to approx 1 1/2cm thick patty.
Re flatten again with palm of hand to approx 1cm thick patty.
Heat oil in a medium frypan and when hot place the pizetti in the hot oil. Once it is golden brown on one side flip over and cook the other side till golden brown.
Remove from pan and place on paper towels to drain the excess oil.
Add cooked sauce topping on top and finish with
grated mozzarella cheese. Serve warm.

Frisa

Make a pitta (refer recipe for Pitta e' Pane) and once cool, cut it in half by slicing through the middle and place in hot pizza oven for 3 hrs until crispy dry.

Rub garlic on dried pitta bread (frisa).

Put frisa on flat plate and pour cold water on top to soak. Don't make it too soft.

Sprinkle oregano on soaked frisa

Heat oil in a fry pan and when hot remove from stove, add paprika, stirring quickly.

Drizzle paprika and oil mixture evenly over frisa

INGREDIENTS
Serves 4 persons

- Half a crispy pitta bread
- 5 spoons of olive oil
- One garlic clove
- 1 full teaspoon of spicy paprika
- 1 teaspoon Oregano

Funci fritti cu Farina

INGREDIENTS
Serves 4 persons

- 1 x 400 gram can button mushrooms

- ½ cup flour

- Oil to fry

Place flour in a shallow dish
Add the mushrooms coating well with flour
Heat a medium size frypan with oil on high heat
Add mushrooms and cook till lightly golden brown
Remove with a slotted spoon and place on paper towel to drain.
Serve as a side dish

Funci sutta olio

Boil vinegar and oil in saucepan
Add mushrooms and cook for 2 minutes.
Drain mushrooms in colander (keep liquid)
And then spread on absorbent paper to cool and dry.

Once dry, mix together with chopped capsicum
And garlic and place in jar.
Add vinegar and oil mixture into jar to cover the mushrooms
Seal jar and place in fridge.
Serve cold.

INGREDIENTS
Makes 500 mls

- 1 litre of white vinegar
- 3/4 cup of olive oil
- 1 tin of button mushrooms sliced
- 1/2 red capsicum small thin slices
- 1 garlic clove thin slices

YOUNG AND OLD..SIDE BY SIDE
NEVER STRANGERS.....
CIAO ZIA !!!

Zio Genio

OLD FRIENDS......NEW AQUANTANCES...
HAND GESTURES
FILL IN THE REAL GUSTO.

LE PINSIERI

THE SUN SETS....

CLAUDIO

AND

THE CHILDREN

WILL BE

HOME SOON....

TOGETHER....

INGREDIENTS
Makes 1000 mls

- 5 tablespoons olive oil.
- 1 medium size onion finely chopped.
- 1 tablespoon of oregano.
- 1 clove of garlic chopped in half.
- Salt or a beef stock cube.
- 4 cans of tomatoes pureed.
- 3/4 cup of water.
- Bunch fresh basil.

NU BELLU SUCU

- 1 oxtail cut into pieces.
- 5 pork ribs.
- 2 pieces of chuck steak.
- 5 tablespoons of olive oil.
- 1 clove of garlic cut in half.
- 1 medium onion finely chopped.
- ¼ cup white wine.
- Salt and pepper.
- 6 cans of tinned tomatoes pureed.
- 500 mls water.
- 1 small bunch of fresh basil.
- 1 tablespoon oregano.

Sucu

Cook on medium heat till onion is translucent.

Add the tomatoes to the saucepan along with the water, stock cube and basil. Bring it to the boil and then the reduce heat and let it simmer for at least an hour or longer or until the sauce has reduced. Keep adding water if it gets too dry.

Nu Bellu Sucu

Heat oil in pan, add onion, garlic and cook for a few minutes.

Add the meats, salt and pepper. Cook the meat and mince till it is browned and cooked through.

Add the wine.

Cook for a few minutes till the wine reduces, then add the pureed tomatoes, water and basil.

Bring to the boil, reduce the heat and simmer for about 2hrs.

If the sauce reduces too quickly keep adding water and taste for seasoning.

Once cooked, remove the chunky pieces of meat, leaving the mince.

Use this sauce for lasagne or any other pasta dish.

Lasagna

Mix flour and eggs in a large bowl and knead until smooth. Cover with cloth and rest for 30 minutes and knead again. Cut into 2 cm thick pieces to pass through pasta machine to make long flat sheets. Start on number 1 and finish on number 5. Lightly sprinkle and spread flour on sheets if too moist. Place on tablecloth and cut into pieces to suit baking dish size. Place 3 cut sheets of pasta at a time into boiling salted water for approximately 1 minute and then transfer into a bowl of cold water for 15 seconds. Remove and place on dry tea towel. Continue the same procedure for the remaining cut sheets.

Have Mince Sauce ready along with grated cheeses and ham to commence layering of the lasagne dish. Spread a small amount of sauce at the bottom of a 4 cm deep baking dish and place first layer of cooked pasta sheets. Lightly cover with more sauce and sprinkle both cheeses and ham. Continue with second layer of pasta, sauce, cheeses and ham. You will need to do 4 layers for a 4cm deep dish. Finish off with final layer of pasta, sauces, cheeses and ham, cover with sheet of baking paper and cover with aluminum foil and place in preheated oven for 30 minutes.

INGREDIENTS
Serves 10 persons

- 250 grms of plain flour
- 2 eggs
- 40 mls of water
- Romano cheese to sprinkle
- Mozzarella cheese to sprinkle
- Sliced ham cut finely to sprinkle
- 1800 mls of "Bellu Sucu" with 250gms of veal mince and 250 gms pork mince.

Follow procedure on page 51 and adding the mince with the meats.

Gnocchi

INGREDIENTS
Serves 6 persons

Place potatoes in a saucepan. Cover with cold water and bring to the boil. Cook for 20-25 minutes or until just tender when tested with a skewer. Drain well. Set aside until just cool enough to handle. While still hot, peel by hand and discard skins. Using a potato ricer puree potatoes into a bowl. Cool slightly.

Add flour to potatoes then use your hands to knead briefly until a soft dough forms. If mixture is still sticky, add a little more flour. Turn dough on to a lightly floured surface.
Cut dough into 4 equal-sized pieces.
Using your hands, gently roll each piece out to form a long roll about 2cm wide. Using a lightly floured knife, cut each roll into 1.5cm-long pieces. Roll each ball of gnocchi over the lines of a lightly-floured gnocchi paddle or fork towards you pressing gently with your index and middle finger to form a dent.

- 6 large desiree potatoes, unpeeled

- 250 gms plain flour

- Salt to taste

- 500 mls Italian Pasta sauce

Bring a large saucepan of salted water to the boil. Add the gnocchi.
As they cook, gnocchi will rise to the surface of the water.
Continue cooking gnocchi at the surface for about a minute then remove with a large slotted spoon and drain well.
Serve immediately, tossed together with pasta sauce.
Notes: To stop starch forming, making gnocchi tough, potatoes need to be mashed very finely.
Older potatoes are better as they release less water

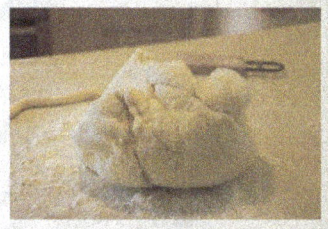

Maccaruni

INGREDIENTS
Serves 12 persons

- 1kg plain flour

- 1 1/2 cups of luke warm water

- 500mls of Italian pasta sauce

Mix flour and water in a bowl
Transfer onto board and knead until firm

Cut into 1 1/5cm pieces and pass through the pasta machine
a few times. Roll into a cylinder (not tight)
Roll the dough by hand into 1cm diameter rope
Cut into 10cm long sections

Press thin cane into centre of cut lengths and roll back and forth
with both hands (don't press to hard) and
gradually spreading hands away from each other to elongate the pasta,
Slide the cane out of the tube of pasta.
Place pasta tube close together on a table cloth and allow
to sit for 15 minutes.

Cook all in pot of salted boiling water
Strain in colander and mix with pasta sauce in a large serving bowl.

56

Cannaloni

INGREDIENTS
Makes 45-50 Cannaloni

(Pasta)
- 1 cup of water
- 1 1/4kg plain flour
- 4 eggs

Or use packet cannelloni tubes

(Meat and spinach)
- ¼ cup of passata
- 1 kg pork mince
- 1 kg yearling
- 2 tablespoons of oil
- 1 small onion grated
- 1 garlic clove crushed
- 250 gms spinach packet
- Pinch of salt

Spinach
Heat 1 tablespoon of oil, add garlic, parsley, salt and pepper and cook for a couple of minutes.

Mince and Spinach filling
Cook onion and garlic, add meat and cook until browned.
Add wine and cook for a few minutes.
Add sauce, passata and spinach.. cook for a few minutes then remove from flame. Add mozzarella, mix until melted and then cool
Add all 3 cheeses and mix all together.
Cool and place in fridge overnight.

Cannelloni Pasta
Beat eggs with water and add flour..rest for 1 to 2 hours
Pass pasta through pasta machine to form thin sheets and cut into 200mm long pieces.
Cook in salted boiling water and then cool then off in cold water
Place meat and spinach on individual pasta sheet and roll (closing off ends on first roll)
 OR......
Cook packet cannelloni tubes in salted boiling water then cool in cold water
Push meat and spinach mixture into cannelloni tube
Place filled tubes into baking dish and layer with pasta sauce.
Cook in oven for 30 minutes.

(Meat and spinach continued :)

. Pinch of salt

. 1/3 cup of parmesan cheese

. 1/3 cup of goat cheese

. 1/3 cup of romano cheese

. Mozzarella cheese 250 grms.

. 1/2 glass of white wine

. 500 mls Pasta sauce

. Spinach. 250 gms

. 1 tablespoon of oil

. 1 clove of garlic crushed

. 1 tablespoon parsley

Pasta al Forno.
Part A...Purpettini

Place all the ingredients in a large bowl and mix thoroughly by hand.
Roll little balls and lightly brown them in a fry pan of hot oil.
Drain onto paper towels, ready to use in Pasta al Forno.

INGREDIENTS
Serves 8 persons

"Purpettini"
- 2 garlic cloves crushed
- 75 gms pork mince
- 75 gms yearling mince
- Pinch of salt
- Parsely 1/4 teaspoons
- 40 gms bread crumbs and 1 egg
- 1/4 cup Romano cheese
- 1/4 teaspoon pepper
- 5 mls milk
- 50 mls water
- Mozzarella cheese 1/2 hand full
- 1/4 cup pasta sauce

Pasta al Forno.
Part B...

Boil salted water for pasta. Cook pasta al dente and place in a colander.

Add thin layer of pasta sauce in the bottom of a baking dish followed by first layer of cooked pasta.

Add small quantities of all the toppings over the pasta and finish off with another layer of pasta sauce.

Start second layer with pasta, repeat toppings and finish off with last layer of pasta sauce.

Place baking paper on top and cover with aluminum foil.

Place in hot oven for approx 30 minutes until cooked.

INGREDIENTS
Serves 8 persons

. 2 eggs
hard boiled

. 250 grms
Rigatoni pasta

. 25 gms
sopressa
finely chopped

. 25 gms bacon
Finely chopped

. Italian sauce
2 cups

. Mozzarella cheese
75 gms

. Romano cheese
75 gms

Lagana e' Ciciri

INGREDIENTS
Serves 4 persons

- 2 Tablespoons olive oil
- 2 cloves garlic sliced thinly
- 1 tablespoon of homemade paprika
- 3 tomatoes, cut in half and grated onto a plate or 3/4 tin of pureed peeled tomatoes
- 1 vegetable stock cube
- 1 cup of water
- 300 grms of dried chickpeas
- 250gms of fresh Lagana
- 1 small bunch of basil

LAGANA
- 1 cup of plain flour
- ¼ cup of water

This makes 250 grams of fresh pasta

Soak dried chickpeas over night in fresh water. Drain and cook in small saucepan with water. Cook for approx 20 minutes (not too soft).
Place the flour in a bowl and make a well in the centre. Add the water and mix together. The mixture will be quite dry but keep mixing and kneading till it all combines (this can take about 10 minutes) Do not add extra water!
Once the mixture has all come together let it sit for ½ an hour. Cut the pasta dough into 4 pieces and pass through the pasta machine starting at number 1 and finishing at number 6. If you prefer it thinner go to number 7.
Pick up one sheet of pasta and pass it through the cutting rollers on the pasta machine making lagana. Place it on a lightly floured tablecloth on a table and let rest till you are ready to use it.
Heat oil in medium saucepan on medium heat and add garlic. Cook slow until garlic is opaque. Add paprika and remove off heat immediately as this burns quickly. Add grated tomato, water, stock cube and chickpeas. Cook for approximately 15 to 20 minutes on simmer and add fresh basil.
Boil water in large saucepan add salt. Add lagana till it's cooked.
Lift the pasta out of the water with tongs and place it in the chickpea mixture. If the dish is too dry add some of the pasta water mix together and serve.
Drain and add to sauce mixture when required.

Lagana e'Fasouli

Soak fresh beans over night in fresh water.
Drain and cook in small saucepan with water.
Cook for approx 20 minutes (not too soft).
Drain and add to sauce mixture when required.

Heat oil in medium saucepan on medium heat and add garlic (cook slow, don't burn) until garlic is opaque.
Add paprika and remove off heat immediately as this burns quickly..
Add grated tomato, water, stock cube and beans. Cook for approximately 15 to 20 minutes on simmer and add fresh basil.

Boil water in large saucepan add salt.
Add fettuccini till it's cooked. Lift the pasta out of the water with tongs and place it in the bean mixture. If the dish is too dry add some of the pasta water mix together and serve.

INGREDIENTS
Serves 6 persons

- Tablespoons olive oil

- 2 cloves garlic sliced thinly

- 1 tablespoon of homemade paprika

- 3 tomatoes cut in half and grated onto a plate or 3/4 peeled tinned tomato can.

- 1 vegetable stock cube

- 1 cup of water

- 300 grms of dryed beans

- 1 packet of fresh fettuccini

- 1 small bunch of basil

Pasta e`Patane

INGREDIENTS
Serves 6 persons

- Basil - 6 leaves
- 1/2 onion, finely chopped
- Pinch of oregano
- 1/2 tin peeled pureed tomatoes
- 4 tablespoons of oil
- 1 teaspoon of salt
- 1 litre of water
- 2 potatoes. Peeled and diced into large cubes
- 1 teaspoon of spicy paprika.

Peel potatoes and cut into 2cm cubes
Heat oil in a saucepan, add onions and cook until the onions are soft
Add oregano, tomatoes, water, basil, salt, paprika into pan. Stir and bring to boil for 1 min.
Add diced potatoes at the boil, close with lid and then turn down heat to simmer for 90 min. In a separate saucepan cook pasta in salted boiling water. Strain when cooked and retain 1 cup of pasta water for later use if final mixture is too dry.
Add strained pasta to potato mixture.
If too dry add a bit of pasta water. Serve hot.

Pasta e` Pisiddri

Heat oil in pan
Add peas, parsley, basil and water. Cook for 30 min until cooked and water is reduced.
Boil water for pasta in separate saucepan add pasta and salt
Once the pasta is cooked, add the cooked peas (with its liquid) into the pasta pan and mix all together.
Allow to sit cook all together for a few minutes before serving.

INGREDIENTS
Serves 4 persons

. 4 tablespoons of olive oil

. 1/2 cup of water to cover peas

. Parsley. Small bunch

. 250 gm packet of peas

. 4 basil leaves

. Salt to taste

. 250 gms of pasta (Tubittini 49. canneroni lisci)

Pasta e' Ciciri

INGREDIENTS
Serves 6 persons

- 2 cups of cooked chick peas
- 4 tablespoons of olive oil
- 3 medium sized tomatoes or 3/4 tin of peeled tomatoes pureed
- 1 large clove of garlic
- 1 teaspoon of paprika
- 3 Basil leaves
- Salt to taste
- 250 gms of pasta of small tube pasta

Place chickpeas with water and pinch of salt in pressure cooker and cook for 15 to 20 min, until chickpeas are cooked. Alternatively soak the chickpeas in water overnight and boil on the stove til tender.

Heat oil in a medium sized saucepan add garlic and cook till opaque.
Add the paprika.
Allow to cook for 1 minute or less as the paprika burns quickly.
Add the tomatoes, pinch of salt and basil.
Bring the sauce to boil for 1 min and then simmer for 45 minutes.

Add the cooked chickpeas to the sauce and simmer for a further 5 mins.
Boil water for pasta in separate pan
On the boil, add pasta and salt
Once the pasta is cooked, drain but reserve a little of the liquid.
Add the pasta to the sauce/chickpea mixture
Allow to cook all together for 1 min. Remove from heat and let rest for 2 minutes before serving.
(It should be of a soup consistency if it is too dry some of the reserve liquid)

Pasta cu Vruocculu

Heat oil in pan and lightly brown the garlic, then add the paprika and stir. (take pan off the heat as paprika burns very quickly)
Add broccoli, water and salt and cook until broccoli are soft, on medium heat with lid on the pan.
Stir occasionally and add a bit more water if too dry.
Slightly crush the broccoli and now it's ready to mix with the cooked spaghetti.

(At the same time as the broccoli are cooking prepare your pasta)
Boil water for pasta in separate pot. On the boil, add pasta and salt
Once the pasta is cooked, drain pasta in a colander
and mix with cooked broccoli in large serving dish.
Mix all together ready for serving.

INGREDIENTS
Serves 4 persons

- 2 heads of broccoli approx 800 gms.
- Salt to taste approx 1 teaspoon
- 1 tablespoon of paprika
- 2 garlic cloves crushed
- 350 gms of spaghetti No 7
- 4 tablespoons of olive oil
- 75 mls of water

Spaghetti cu aglia, olio e` sinisu

INGREDIENTS
Serves 4 persons

- 350 gms dried spaghetti
- ½ cup of olive oil
- 3 large garlic cloves crushed
- 1 large garlic clove thin sliced
- 1 table spoon of paprika

Cook spaghetti in salted boiling water.

Heat oil in saucepan and add both crushed and sliced garlic. Reduce heat to low and stir in garlic and cook until it starts to turn clear.
Remove from heat, add paprika and mix through.

Drain spaghetti and place in serving dish, then pour garlic, oil and paprika mixture over the spaghetti.

Mix through thoroughly and serve immediately.

Pastina

Place the ingredients except the pastina in a medium sized saucepan and cover with water.
Bring to the boil then reduce the heat and let simmer for about 1 hour or until the liquid is reduced and the chicken and vegetables are cooked.

Cook the pastina in a boiling salted water till pasta is cooked.
Strain the pastina and place into a bowl or another saucepan.
Strain the broth of the soup mixture and add it to the pastina.

INGREDIENTS
Serves 4 persons

. 2 chicken legs or carcass of a chicken.
any kind is fine, it should have bones.

. 1 large ripe tomato

. 1 onion

. 1 carrot

. 1 chicken stock cube or salt

. Small bunch of parsley

. ¼ of small pasta (pastina) risoni or similar type

IL CORTILE

DISTANT
MEMORIES LINGURE..
ONLY CHILDRENS
LAUGHING ECHOS
REMAIN...
WHEN
MAMMA CALLS
FOR
LUNCH....

NARROW PASSAGES LEAD TO LIVELY ENTRANCES... SUPRISES AROUND THE CORNER...

ABANDONED......
BUT NOT FORGOTTEN

TOOLS LIE
RESTING...
WAITING..
SPRING WILL
ARRIVE
SOON...

NEVER DISCARDED....
THEIR TIME
WILL
COME.

LA FONTANA

FROM HIGH
IN THE
MOUNTAINS
WATER FLOWS....
A CHANCE
MEETING
WITH FRIENDS...
AQUA
FILLS INTO
TERRACOTTA
VESSILS

VIBRANT COLOURS AND TEXTURES...
ALL ADDING THEIR MIX IN TIME.....

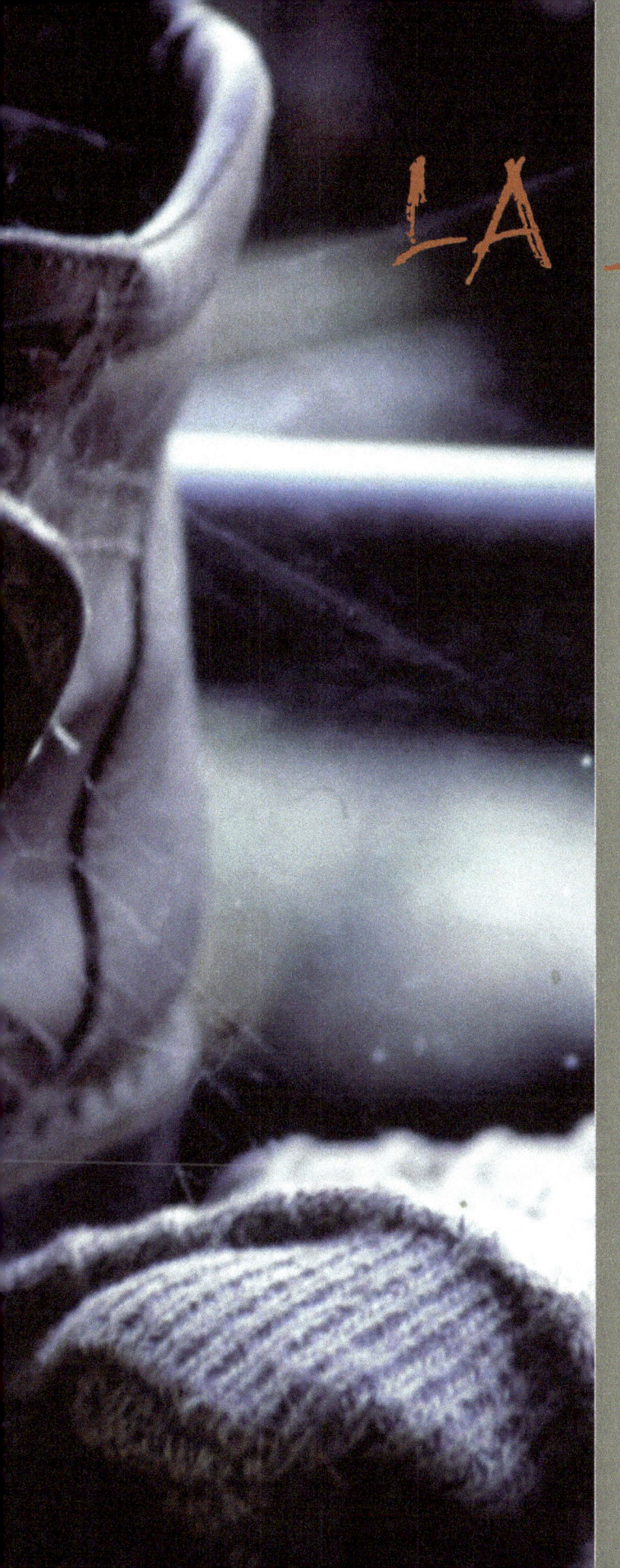

LA SCARPA

They walked
to many
beats...
Sunday church....
In the fields...
Dancing....
Life
was
good....

Baccala cu Brodo di Patane

INGREDIENTS
Serves 4 persons

- 4 tablespoons of olive oil
- Half onion chopped finely
- 1/4 teaspoon Oregano
- 3/4 tin of peeled tomatoes
- Salt to taste
- 2 peeled potatoes cut into quarters
- 4 pieces of Baccala
- Heaped tablespoon of paprika
- 1 1/2 cups of water

Start by making the sauce.

Heat oil in pan
Add onions and cook until soft
Add tomatoes, oregano and salt

Cook for 30 min
Add potatoes, baccala, paprika and water

Cook for 60 min

Lenticchie

Soak lentils in fresh water overnight in bowl..
enough water to cover plus a bit more.
Place olive oil, onion, tomatoes, garlic and chicken stock in
saucepan and cook for 20 minutes on low heat.
Stir occasionally. Add lentils, basil and water to cover plus
 extra 4 cm of water above.
Bring to the boil for 2 min and add paprika and salt,
stir and reduce heat..Simmer for 75 minutes.
Stir occasionally.
Dish is cooked once lentils are soft

INGREDIENTS
Serves 4 persons

. 1 Small onion finely diced

. 1 clove garlic crushed

. 2 ripe tomatoes, peeled and blended or 3/4 can of peeled tomatoes

. 4 tablespoons of olive oil

. 1 cup of lentils

. Small bunch of basil

. 1 chicken stock cube

. 1 tablespoon of spicy paprika.

. Salt to taste

Minestra di Patane

INGREDIENTS
Serves 6 persons

- Basil - 6 leaves
- 1/2 onion, finely chopped
- Pinch of oregano
- 1 tin peeled pureed tomatoes
- 4 tablespoon of oil
- 1 teaspoon of salt
- 1 litre of water
- 2 1/2 potatoes. Peeled and diced into large cubes
- 1 teaspoon of spicy paprika.

Peel potatoes and cut into 2cm cubes
Heat oil in pan, add onions and cook until the onions are soft
Add oregano, tomatoes, water, basil, salt and paprika.

Stir and bring to boil for 1 min.
Add diced potatoes and place lid on the saucepan.

Turn down heat to simmer for 90 min.
Serve hot when potatoes are cooked.

Pisiddri

Place oil in a saucepan on medium heat and add diced onions.
Cook till onions are translucent.
Add peas, salt and water.
Make sure the water level is just enough to cover the peas.
Cover with lid and bring to the boil then reduce to simmer.
for 15 to 20 minutes or until the peas are soft and cooked.

INGREDIENTS
Serves 4 persons

. 2 tablespoons of olive oil

. 1 small onion, diced finely

. 4 cups of peas

. Salt to taste

. 1 cup of water

Risotto cu Mince

INGREDIENTS
Serves 4 persons

- 500 grams mince
- 1 medium onion finely diced
- 1 clove of garlic cut into half
- 2 tablespoons of olive oil
- Pinch of salt
- 1/4 cup white wine
- 1 cup of Arborio rice
- 1/3 cup grated Romano cheese
- 1 flat teaspoon of curry powder
- 2 large tomatoes or 3 medium ones cut in half and the insides grated
- 1 tablespoon of finely chopped Italian parsley
- 1 beef stock cube dissolved in a litre of boiling water

Heat oil in saucepan, add onion and garlic and cook for about one Minute. Add the mince and brown well.
Once mince is nicely browned salt the mince and add the curry powder, cook for 2 minutes.
Squash the lumps out with a wooden spoon until it is loose.

Add the grated tomato and cook for a few minutes Add the wine, cook for a further 2 minutes then add the rice stirring continuously until all combined and rice is lightly browned. Gradually add beef stock (dissolved in water) one cup at a time stirring continuously on medium to low heat.
(This takes approx 20-25 minutes)

When the cup of stock has been absorbed add another; keep doing this until all the stock is absorbed and the rice is soft and tender. Remove off the heat and stir in the Romano cheese, sprinkle with chopped parsley and serve immediately.

Verdura cu Patane e sinisu

Shred and chop the silver beet into small pieces.
Boil water in pot and add silver beet and salt to taste.
Bring to boil and cook for 10 minutes, then strain into a colander.

Place chopped potatoes into pot with water.
Bring to boil and add 1/4 teaspoon of salt.
Once cooked cut potatoes into thick slices

Heat a pan with 4 teaspoons of oil and 2 cloves of garlic
and slowly brown, then add 3/4 teaspoons of paprika and stir.
(Note: Paprika cooks very quickly and will burn after 10 seconds.)
Quickly add the silver beet and 3/4 cup of water.
Cook for 10 minutes and then add the potatoes.

Mix all together and add 1 teaspoon of oil if too dry.
Mix well and serve.

INGREDIENTS
Serves 4 persons

- 1 bunch of silver beet
- 1 1/2 tea spoons of salt
- 1 large potato cut into quarters
- 2 tea spoons of paprika
- 2 cloves of garlic cut in halves
- 3/4 cup of water

Insalada di Vruoccucli

INGREDIENTS
Serves 4 persons

. 2 small heads
   of broccoli
    cut into
    flowerets

. 2 cloves of garlic
   thinly sliced.

. 2 tablespoons
   of olive oil

. 1 teaspoon
   of salt

. 1 teaspoon
   of red
   wine vinegar

Boil water in saucepan and add broccoli and teaspoon of salt.
Cook for 5 minutes.
Drain in colander.
Place broccoli in bowl and add garlic, oil, and red wine vinegar.
Mix all together and place in fridge and serve cold.

Vruoccucli alla Tieddra

INGREDIENTS
Serves 4 persons

Cut broccoli into florets.
Bring a large saucepan to the boil with salt and add broccoli.
Cook for 5 minutes and drain in colander.
Oil base of baking dish and place 1 layer cooked broccoli
Sprinkle cheese, finely chopped garlic and bread crumbs and paprika.
Start next layer with more broccoli, cheese, garlic and
bread crumbs and paprika.
Finish off by sprinkling paprika and drizzle of olive oil.
Add water along the edges of the dish.

Cover with baking paper and aluminum foil and
place in 180 deg oven for 30 min.

- 2 small heads of broccoli cut into florets
- 2 medium cloves of garlic sliced
- 2 tablespoons of olive oil for drizzling each layer
- 2 teaspoons of paprika
- 4 tablespoons bread crumbs
- 2 tablespoons of water

Zucchini di Papá

INGREDIENTS
Serves 6 persons

. 1 small onion diced.

. 4 tablespoons of oil

. 1 large zucchini - 500 gms

. 2 ripe tomatoes halved and then grated.

. 1 vegetable stock cube

. 1 tablespoon chopped parsley

. 1 tablespoon chopped basil

. Water - enough to cover zucchini

. Sprig of oregano

. 1 teaspoon of spicy paprika

In a medium sized pan, heat oil on medium heat.
Add onions and cook until they turn transparent.
Add grated tomato, fresh basil and fresh parsley.
Cook for approx 10 minutes on low heat and stir.
Scoop away and discard some of the inside flesh of zucchini
Cut zucchini into thin slices.

Place chopped zucchini and stock cube into the pot
Add enough water to just cover zucchini and stir.
Bring to the boil.
Reduce heat and simmer until zucchini is cooked soft and tender and liquid reduced. Stir occasionally.

Minestrone

Cut all vegetables into small cubes and place in a large pot.
Bring to the boil and simmer for 2 hours. Stir occasionally
Add more water if reducing too quickly.
Serve hot.

INGREDIENTS
Serves 6 persons

. All ingredients are finely chopped.
. 4 carrots
. 1 cup of green beans
. 1 small sweet potato
. 1/4 cabbage
. 1 large potato
. 2 tomatoes pureed
. 1 large onion
. 2 cloves of garlic, crushed
. 1 small head of broccoli
. 1 tablespoon of parsley
. 1 stick of celery
. 1/2 red capsicum
. 1 small zucchini
. 3 chicken stock cubes

. 3 tablespoons of oil
. Salt to taste
. Water to cover

Insalata di Pomodoro

INGREDIENTS
Serves 4 persons

- 3 medium firm ripe tomatoes.
- Half red onion.
- 5 basil leaves.
- Sprinkle of oregano.
- Salt to taste.
- 2 tablespoons virgin olive oil.

Cut tomatoes into pieces by holding the tomato in your hand and letting the tomatoes fall into the small bowl.
Cut onion into quarters then slice thinly add to tomatoes.
Drizzle olive oil, sprinkle with salt and sprinkle dried oregano and basil.
Mix and serve with crusty Italian bread

Insalata di Tonno e` Pomodoro

Cut tomatoes into pieces by holding the tomato in your hand and letting the tomatoes fall into the small bowl.

Add tuna from can along with its oil.
Cut onion into quarters then slice, add to tomatoes.
Cut basil into thin strips and add to tomatoes.
Drizzle olive oil, and sprinkle salt to taste.

Mix and serve with crusty Italian bread

INGREDIENTS
Serves 4 persons

- 3 medium firm ripe tomatoes.
- Half a red onion thinly sliced
- 2 cans of Tuna in oil 95 gms cans
- 5 basil leaves.
- Salt to taste.
- 2 tablespoons virgin olive oil.

Frittata di Cipuddra

INGREDIENTS
Serves 4 persons

. 2 large white onions.
  Cut into thin slices

. 5 eggs whisked.

. 5 table spoons of
  olive oil

. Salt to taste

Cook onions in frypan on low heat in oil
until soft, translucent and almost caramelized

Add small pinch of salt on onions
Add small pinch of salt to eggs and whisk
Add eggs to pan and cook on one side.
Flip omelette onto large flat plate
and slide back into pan. (cooked side up) to
cook the other side or alternatively place under grill
Cook until golden brown
Slide onto serving plate.

Frittata di Pipazzi

Slice the capsicum into thin long strips
Heat oil in a medium size frypan on medium heat
Add the capsicum and sprinkle with salt.
Reduce the heat to low so the capsicum cooks slowly
until it is very soft.
In the meantime whisk the eggs in a bowl with a pinch of salt.
Once the capsicum is nice and soft and almost caramelized
 add the eggs and increase the heat to medium.
Cook the frittata on one side.
When cooked on one side remove from the heat and if you are
able to, place a clean flat plate on the top of the frittata and flip
it over onto the frypan so the other side can cook.
Alternatively place the frypan in the oven so the top
of the frittata can finish cooking.

INGREDIENTS
Serves 4 persons

- 5 long Italian capsicums or 2 large capsicums. red or green or both

- 5 eggs

- Oil to cover the bottom of a medium size frypan

Patane e` Pipazzi

INGREDIENTS
Serves 4 persons

- 3 medium sized potatoes
- Olive oil
- 5 long red Italian Capsicums or your ordinary Red capsicums
- Salt to taste

Peel potatoes and cut into thin slices. 3mm thick.
Remove most of the seeds and cut capsicums into thin strips.
Heat oil in a frying pan and cook the capsicums first until semi cooked, then add potato slices and salt.
Cook on low heat until potatoes are soft.

Pipazzi arrustuti

INGREDIENTS
Serves 4 persons

Slowly roast the capsicum over hot coals for approximately 15 minutes until they are soft and collapse.
Remove the outer charred skin off the capsicum.
Cut roasted capsicums in thin strips and place in a bowl.

Add the remaining ingredients and mix to combine ready for serving.

If storing in the fridge, place the capsicum in a jar and cover with vegetable oil.

. 4 large capsicums

. 2 clove of garlic

. Salt to taste

. 3 tablespoons of olive oil

. ½ dried oregano

Favi

INGREDIENTS
Serves 4 persons

- 2 tablespoons of olive oil
- 1 small onion, diced finely
- 2 cups of broad beans
- Salt to taste
- 1 cup of water

Place oil in a saucepan on medium heat and add diced onions.
Cook till onions are translucent.
Add broad beans, salt and water.
Make sure water level is just enough to cover the broad beans.
Cover with lid and bring to the boil then reduce to simmer.
for 15 to 20 minutes or until the broad beans are soft and cooked.

Insalata di Fasuoli

Top and tail ends of beans
Place into pot of boiling water until cooked
(10min approx)
Once cooked remove and place in colander to cool
Dress with oil, vinegar, garlic and salt.
Place in fridge to cool and serve cold.

INGREDIENTS
Serves 4 persons

- 150 gms of green beans
- Pinch of salt
- 1 clove of chopped garlic. Not too thin.
- 1 teaspoon of white vinegar
- 2 tablespoons of olive oil

La Campagna

TIME PASSES
SLOWLY
NEVER
A
RUSH....

ALWAYS
TOMORROW

FARMHOUSES DOT
THE SURROUNDING HILLS......
SHORT STROLL TO TOWN...
NEVER DISTANT..
READY FOR ANY OCCASION.....

NOTHING IS HIDDEN.....
ROUGHNESS DELIGHTS AS YOU
MEANDER PAST....

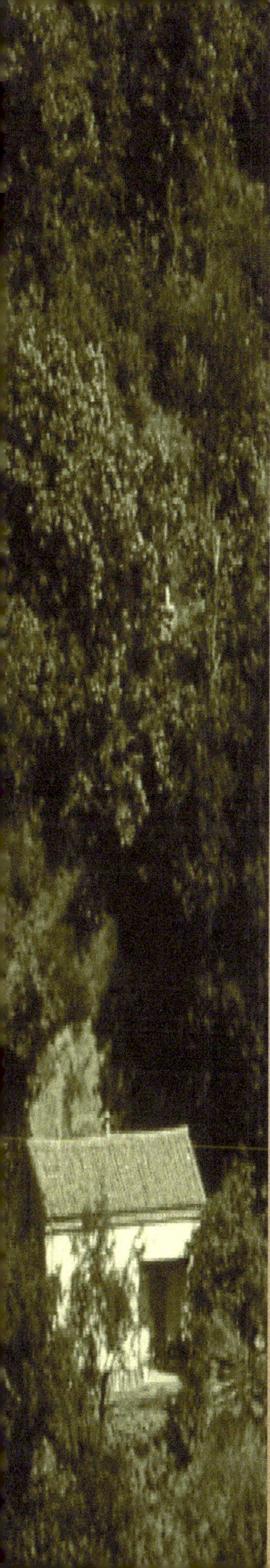

Pitticeddri di Riso

INGREDIENTS
Makes 12 Pitticeddri

- 2 cups of rice medium grain

- 1 tablespoon of parsley, finely chopped

- 3/4 cup of grated Romano cheese

- 2 fresh eggs

- 1 egg for coating beaten.

- Bread crumbs to roll in

- Salt to taste for the rice

- Vegetable oil for frying

Cook rice in boiling salted water. Once cooked, place rice in a mixing bowl and put in the fridge to cool.
Once cool remove from fridge and
add parsley, salt, cheese and 2 eggs.
Mix by hand.
Beat the remaining egg in a small bowl to coat the made pittichedri

Place 2 heaped handfuls of bread crumbs onto baking paper.
Grab a small handful of mixture and roll into a
3cm dia by 10cm long roll.
Roll pittichedri in egg mix, and roll into bread crumbs until the whole pittichedri is covered.

Heat oil in small deep pan, (enough to cover the pittichedri)
Cook 4 pittichedri at a time until golden brown on the outside.

Remove with a slotted spoon and place on paper towels.
Place onto plate for final serving

115

Pitticeddri di Patane

INGREDIENTS
Makes 12 patties

- 6 potatoes peeled

- 1 tablespoon of parsley, finely chopped

- 1 tablespoon of salt

- 3/4 cup of grated Romano cheese

- 1 fresh egg

- 1 egg beaten for coating.

- Bread crumbs to coat patties

- Salt to taste

- Vegetable oil for frying

Boil potatoes till just cooked.
Mash potatoes
Cool till tepid
Add remaining ingredients.
Shape into long tubes.
Roll in beaten egg then roll in breadcrumbs.
Deep fry till golden brown.

Pitticeddri di Vruoccucli

Same procedure can be used for Cauliflower.

INGREDIENTS
Serves 6 persons

- Large head of Broccoli
- 1 egg
- 1 heaped teaspoon of finely chopped parsley.
- 2 heaped tablespoons of Romano cheese.
- 3 heaped tablespoons of plain flour.
- 3 heaped tablespoons of self-rasing flour.
- 150mls of water
- Vegetable oil for frying
- Pinch of salt

Break broccoli head into flowerets and place into large saucepan with enough water to cover.
Bring to the boil on high heat and cook for approximately 3 minutes, then drain into a colander and allow to cool.
Put all the ingredients in a bowl and mix until all combined.
Heat vegetable oil in a frying pan. Dip each individual broccoli by hand into the mixture and place into hot pan.
Cook each side until golden brown.
Remove from the pan and allow excess oil to drain onto paper towels.
Continue the process for the remaining broccoli.
Serve either warm or cold.

Pitticeddri di Yuri

INGREDIENTS
Serves 6 persons

- 12 Zucchini flowers
- 1 fresh egg
- 1 Teaspoon finely chopped parsley
- 3/4 cup of water
- 3/4 cup of plain flour
- 1 tablespoon self raising flour
- Vegetable oil for frying

Start with making batter by mixing both flours, egg and parsley with water in a bowl.

Wash zucchini flowers and individually dip into batter and then deep fry in pan with hot oil.

Turn each patty over when golden brown and cook the other side.
Place on absorbent paper to drain excess oil.
Serve warm.

Mulangiana alla Parmigiana

Prepare eggplant patties as shown on page 123.
(Pittichedri di Mulangiana). Pour a bit of Suco on the
bottom of a suitable sized baking dish and place how
ever many patties you want as a single layer into the dish.
Sprinkle the cheese over the patties and pour the remaining
Suco over the top
Cover the dish with layer of baking paper and seal with aluminium foil.
Place in a pre heated oven to 200 deg and cook for approx 30min

INGREDIENTS
Allow for 2 patties per person

- Pre-made eggplant Patties (page 123)
- 250 mls of Italian pasta sauce (Suco) (page 51)
- Hand full of grated mozzarella cheese

Pitticeddri di Mulangiana

INGREDIENTS

Serves 4 persons

- 4 large eggplants or 8 small ones
- Salt
- 2 large cloves of garlic
- 1/3 cup finely grated Romano cheese
- 1/3 cup finely chopped Italian parsley
- 1/3 cup grated Philadelphia frozen cheese. freeze the Philadelphia cheese before you grate it
- 6 slices of day old Vienna bread (breadcrumbs)
- 1 egg
- 1 egg yolk

Cut eggplant into slices and salt.
Bring water to boil in a large saucepan
Add cut and salted eggplant
Boil until tender
Remove from stove, drain eggplant in colander until eggplant has cooled
While eggplant is still in colander press with a fork to remove excess water.
Turn eggplant onto a board and chop finely
Place eggplant in a large bowl add parsley, garlic, eggs cheeses and fresh breadcrumbs
Mix with hands to combine making sure you "squeeze" the ingredients and form into flat oval patties
Either shallow fry or grill in oven until lightly golden brown

Minestra di Mulangiana

Heat oil in a saucepan; add the onion, capsicum and garlic; cook till onion is soft.
 Add the tomatoes, eggplant, water and basil.
Check for salt and add more if necessary.
Bring to the boil then reduce the heat to simmer and let cook slowly for approximately 30 mins or until the eggplant is very tender.
Remove from the stove and add the grated cheese.
Serve with crusty bread.

INGREDIENTS
Serves 6 persons

- 3 medium sized eggplants cut into strips, then salt
- 4 tablespoons of olive oil
- 1 small onion thinly sliced
- ½ red capsicum thinly sliced
- 1 clove of garlic thinly sliced
- 3 large ripe tomatoes finely chopped or grated
- 2 tablespoons of grated Romano cheese
- 6 fresh basil leaves
- 1 cup of water
- Salt to taste

IL PRATO

Short black coffee.....
Buon giorno!
Then
the
day
begins

ALBERI D'OLIVE

The olive harvest
is near...
Sweet...
thick...
Virgin oil drizzled
on fresh
baked bread...
Um....
buono..

HIS SMALL OLIVE GROVE
BRINGS JOY......
HARD WORK
AND CONTENTMENT....

LA CASTAGNA

Warmth by the fireplace....
Chestnuts roasting....
Red wine and grappa...
Too cold outside...
No work tomorrow...

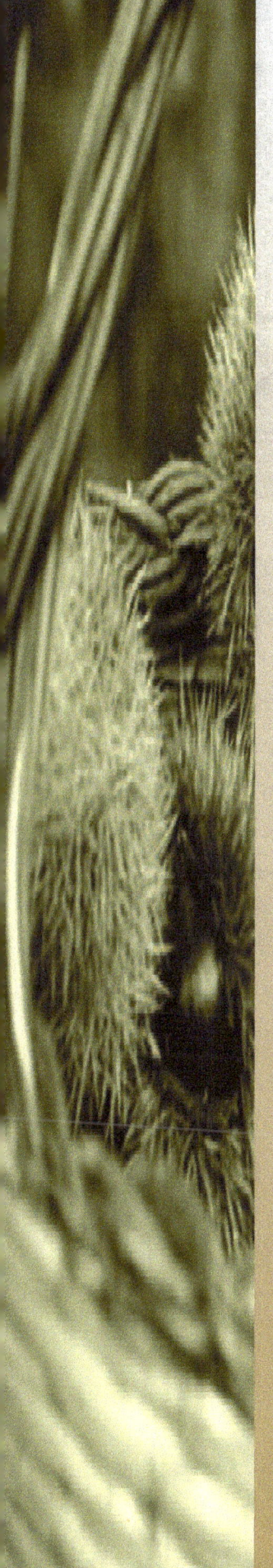

THE MOUNTAINS BECOME ALIVE......
THE CHESTNUT HARVEST HAS BEGUN......

Vrascioli

INGREDIENTS
8 Pieces

- 8 pieces of chicken thighs

- 2 tablespoons of parsley finely chopped

- 1 tablespoon of oregano

- 2 cloves of crushed garlic

- Salt to season

- 1/4 cup finely grated Romano cheese

- 8 thin slices of pancetta or prosciutto

- ½ cup of white wine

- 2 tablespoons olive oil

To make herb mixture, place parsley, oregano and garlic in a small bowl, mix to combine.
Spread each chicken thigh out on a board and gently pound to flatten out. (careful not to break the chicken)
Sprinkle on some salt to taste
(not too much - prosciutto is quite salty)
Sprinkle some of the herb mixture on each thigh followed by a sprinkling of Romano cheese.
Place a piece of prosciutto on top.
Roll each chicken thigh up tightly and hold together with toothpicks
Heat the oil in a frying pan and fry the rolls over high heat until they are brown all over.
(don't overcook them as they will be finished off in the oven)
Place browned chicken thighs into a lightly oiled baking pan.
Add the white wine and a final drizzle of olive oil over each thigh.
Place in a 200 deg oven for 30 minutes.

Porkbelly Vrascioli

Remove the skin and fat off the porkbelly and then score the porkbelly so it lays flat and will be easy to roll.

Lay out porkbelly and evenly spread garlic, parsley oregano, cheese and panchetta.
Roll the porkbelly into a tight roll and tie off with cooking string along the full length and width.
Prepare hot oil in frypan and sear the rolled up porkbelly Vrasciola evenly on all sides.

Place Italian sauce (Suco) into large pot and bring to the boil. Add the seared Vrasciola and cook for approx 60 minutes on simmer. Once cooked remove the string and cut Vrasciola into 2cm thick rolls and serve.

INGREDIENTS
Serves 6 persons

- 1 x Porkbelly
- Approximztely 5 thin slices of proscuitto.
- 1 teaspoon of chopped parsley
- Pinch of oregano
- 1 clove crushed garlic
- 2 tablespoons grated Romano or percorino cheese
- Sprinkle of Salt and pepper
- Cooking string
- 1 - 1.5 Litres of Suco

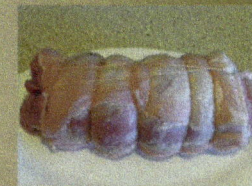

Cotaletti

INGREDIENTS
Makes approx 8 pieces

- 500 grams of thinly cut round steak or yearling or topside or veal
- can be substituted with chicken fillets
- 2 eggs
- Sprinkle salt on each cutlet.
- 2 tablespoons finely chopped parsley
- 1 teaspoon apple cider vinegar
- 2 cups of breadcrumbs
- 1 cup of olive oil for frying

Place eggs in bowl, add salt and vinegar and beat for a few minutes with a fork. Add parsley. Sprinkle steak with salt. Place all of the steak into the egg mixture and mix with clean hands to combine. Place in fridge for ½ hour or longer to tenderize the meat. (overnight is even better)

Spread the breadcrumbs out in a large plate.
Lay each steak in the breadcrumbs and press down.
Turn over and repeat.
Place crumbed steak onto a clean plate.

Heat the oil in a large frying pan and add steaks a few at a time making sure they don't overlap. Cook one side till deep golden brown then turn over to cook the other side.
Remove from pan and drain on paper towels. Serve warm.

Carna alla Pizzaiola

Heat oil on high in a frying pan and sear all the meat slices and remove from frying pan onto a plate.

Sprinkle seared meat with salt

Place one layer of seared meat in large frypan and add garlic, parsley, tomatoes, cheese and oregano on top. Place second layer of seared meat on top and repeat previous procedure.

Put lid on top of pan and cook on medium heat for 30 minutes and then mix all together at the end. Serve in the pan.

INGREDIENTS
Serves 6 persons

- 8 pieces of yearling rump approx 1 Kg
- 2 garlic cloves finely chopped
- 2 tablespoons parsley
- 2 tablespoons Olive oil
- 3 tomatoes Chopped roughly
- Salt to taste
- 4 tablespoons grated Romano cheese
- 1 teaspoon oregano

INGREDIENTS
Serves 6 persons

. 500 gms of veal mince

. 500 gms of pork mince

. 2 heaped tablespoons of chopped parsley

. 2 cloves of crushed garlic

. 300 gms of fresh white bread crumbs

. 3/4 cup of grated Romano cheese

. pinch of Pepper

. 1 flat tablespoon of salt

. 3 fresh eggs

. 3 tablespoons of cooked Italian tomato sauce (page 51)

. 1/2 cup of water

. Olive oil for frying

Purrpetti

Place all the above ingredients into a large mixing bowl and mix by hand until all the ingredients are blended together.

By hand roll and turn a small amount of mixture into a 40 dia ball.
After all the balls are made, fry them in oil until golden brown on all sides.

Finish cooking browned meat balls in Italian tomato sauce for 45 minutes on simmer
Once cooked, remove them from sauce and serve in bowl.

Purrputunu

SAUCE
Heat oil in a medium sized pan. Add garlic and cook till it is opaque. Add the remaining ingredients and bring to the boil for 1 minute. Reduce the heat then simmer for 30 minutes.

PURRPUTUNU
Boil 2 eggs in a small saucepan for 10 mins.
Peel when cooked and set aside.
Place all the remaining ingredients into a large mixing bowl and mix by hand until they are blended together.

By hand roll and turn the whole meat mixture into a 10cm diameter long roll. Slightly flatten out the meat mixture and place both hard boiled eggs in the middle.
Re shape the meat mixture back into the roll shape, making sure all the eggs are covered up. Sear the finished meat in an oiled pan, on all sides.

Once seared place in baking dish with Italian tomato sauce, place a couple of sliced tomatoes on top to keep moist, cover with aluminium foil and bake in a hot oven for 45 minutes.
Once cooked, remove it from the sauce, cut into slices and serve.

INGREDIENTS
Serves 6 persons

- 500 gms of veal mince
- 500 gms of pork mince
- 2 heaped tablespoons of chopped parsley
- 2 cloves of crushed garlic
- 300 gms of fresh white bread crumbs
- 3/4 cup of grated Romano cheese
- pinch of Pepper
- 1 flat tablespoon of salt
- 3 fresh eggs
- 3 tablespoons of cooked Italian tomato sauce (page 51)
- 1/2 cup of water
- Olive oil for frying

SAUCE
- 4 tablespoons. Olive oil
- 3 large tomatoes or 1 can of tinned tomatoes
- 1 large clove of garlic chopped.
- 4 basil leaves
- 1/2 beef stock cube
- 1/4 cup of water
- Salt to taste

Savuzizza Calabrese

INGREDIENTS
Serves 6 persons

- 1 Kg pork mince
- 1 teaspoon of fennel seeds
- Pinch of black pepper
- Pinch of salt
- 1 tablespoon of paprika

Mix the pork mince and all the ingredients in a bowl. Pass the mixture through a sausage machine and tie off each sausage at approximately 10 cm.

Heat pan with olive oil and add sausages. Keep turning the sausages until cooked and browned on all sides and ready for serving.
Sausages can also be cooked in the oven by placing the sausages in an oiled baking tray and into a preheated oven at 200 deg.

Keep turning the sausages until cooked and browned on all sides ready for serving.

Rapi e` Savuzizza

Heat oil in frypan, add chopped sausage and cook till sausage is crispy.

Add rapi, paprika and salt.
Cook till rapi are tender.

Add a little water if mixture is too dry.

INGREDIENTS
Serves 4 persons

. 250 grams of Rapi

. 3 tablespoons of olive oil

. Paprika. 1 teaspoon

. Salt to taste

. 8 Italian sausages cut into bite sized pieces.
 (refer page 149)

Pollo arrustutu

INGREDIENTS
Serves 6 persons

- 1 x whole chicken cut into pieces
- 1 x cup of Flour
- 3 x eggs
- 3 cups of breadcrumbs
- Salt to taste

In a bowl whisk eggs with some salt
Add the chicken and let sit for as long as possible in the fridge (overnight if possible)

Place the flour in a plastic bag add the chicken and shake the bag around so the chicken is well coated in the flour.
Remove chicken pieces and place in the egg mixture.
In another bowl add the breadcrumbs.
Place the chicken pieces one by one in the breadcrumbs coating well and patting with your hand so the crumbs cling to the chicken.

In a medium to large frypan heat the oil on high heat and cook chicken pieces till golden brown. Place the cooked chicken pieces in a large baking dish which has been coated with a small amount of olive oil and then drizzle a small amount of oil on top.

Cover the chicken with alfoil and bake in a moderate oven for about 45 mins to 1 hour or till the chicken is cooked through and not pink.

Ficutu e` Pipazzi

Heat oil in a medium sized frying pan;
add the capsicum, garlic and salt.

Cook till capsicum is just turning soft.

Add the chicken livers, oregano and a little bit of salt.
Cook until the livers are cooked through.

INGREDIENTS
Serves 3 persons

. 250grams organic chicken livers roughly chopped

. 1 large red capsicum halved then sliced

. 5 tablespoons olive oil

. 2 cloves of garlic sliced

. 1 teaspoon dried oregano

. Salt to taste

THE AIR IS FILLED WITH THE SWEET AROMA OF FRESH CHEESE... SALAMI... AND MARKET CHATTER

IL MERCATO

A LEASURELY STROLL
WITH FRIENDS....
CLOTHES...
FOOD..
THE MARKETS OFFER IT ALL.

SEARCHING FOR BARGAINS......

....WHILST OTHERS ATTEND TO OTHER MATTERS.

Canolli

INGREDIENTS
50 canolli

- 2 cups of plain flour
- 40 gms of lard
- 1 tablespoon of Caster sugar
- 1 egg
- ½ cup of Cinzano Bianca
- ¼ teaspoon of grated cinnamon quills
- 1 tablespoon of icing sugar
- Oil for deep frying.
- Metal cylinders

Mix flour, caster sugar, lard, egg and Cinzano by hand with finger tips… keep mixing till combined then knead until smooth.

Cut mixture into 10cm sq pieces 1cm thick and start passing it through a pasta machine. Start on No 1; keep folding the dough sheet and increase the pasta machine setting to N3, until the dough sheet is like velvet. The sheet should be approx 3 ½ cm wide to suit the metal cylinders. Repeat for the remaining dough.

Roll the sheet onto a metal cannoli cylinder and cut the end to make a full revolution.

Seal the ends with water and press firmly to stick both ends together. Add oil and lard into small deep frying pan and bring to the boil. Place finished cannoli cylinder (the dough wrapped on the outside) into the boiling oil until golden brown. (2 min approx) Place vertically on a tray lined with absorptent paper, when slightly cooled, remove the inner metal cylinder.

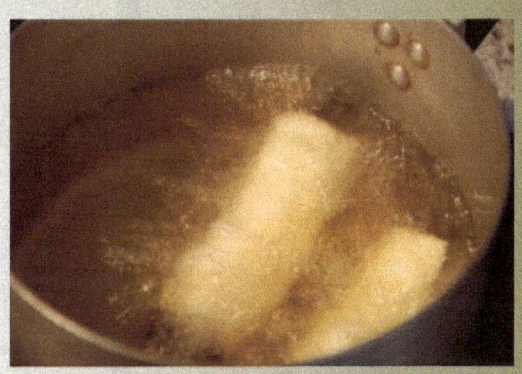

Mix icing sugar and grated cinnamon in a small dish.
Once cool to touch fill each cannoli with authentic white or
chocolate Italian cream.(refer recipe. Page 177/178)
Place on serving tray and sprinkle with icing sugar
and cinnamon mixture through sieve. Place in fridge to cool ... serve cold

Biscotti Lungi

INGREDIENTS
Makes approx 50 biscuits

(Biscuit Mixture)
- 1 tin of condensed milk
- 5 eggs
- 2 teaspoons vanilla extract
- 1 lemon zest
- 4 cups SR flour

(Coating Mixture)
- 2 cups of sugar
- 1/2 cup of water
- 1 lemon zest

Place condensed milk, lemon zest and eggs into bowl and beat with electric mixer for 5 minutes.
Add sifted flour and stir with wooden spoon until smooth.
Place some flour on a wooden board (for mixture not to stick).
Place some of the mixture on the board and roll with your hands into a 1 1/2 cm diameter roll. Cut roll into 8 cm mm long pieces and place on tray lined with baking paper.
Leave sufficient gaps between the biscuits for the biscuits to spread.
Place in 200 deg oven for approx 10 min, until golden brown
Allow to cool on tablecloth and shake off excess flour.

In a saucepan add sugar, water and lemon zest. Bring to the boil and stir until the sugar is dissolved. Place biscuits in large bowl and pour in hot coating mixture, stirring with a wooden spoon, being careful not to break the biscuits.
Mix until all the biscuits are coated well. Allow to cool and serve.

Biscotti di Mamma

Place butter, sugar and eggs into bowl and beat.
Then add vanilla and Cinzano and keep beating until the sugar is dissolved. Add sifted flour and stir with wooden spoon until combined.

Place some flour on a wooden board (for mixture not to stick)
Place some of the mixture on the board and roll with your hands into a 2cm diameter piece. Cut biscuits into 12cm long pieces and place on tray lined with baking paper.
Leave sufficient gaps between the biscuits for the biscuits to spread.
Brush the biscuits with egg and finish with sprinkling of white sugar.

Place in 200 deg oven for approx 10 min, until golden brown
Allow to cool on wire tray.

INGREDIENTS
Makes approx 40 biscuits

- 6 eggs
- 250 grams of softened butter
- 1 cup of sugar
- 2 teaspoons vanilla extract
- 1 lemon zest
- 4 ¼ cups Self raising flour
- 1 tablespoon Cinzano liquor
- Extra egg for brushing biscuits.
- Extra sugar for sprinkling on biscuits.

INGREDIENTS
Makes 40 biscuits

- 3 eggs

- 3/4 cup of white sugar

- 125 gms of softened butter.

- 3 teaspoons of vanilla essence

- 1/2 lemon peel grated

- 380 grms of self raising flour (sifted)

- 110 grms icing sugar

Biscotti cu Pinozzi

Heat oven to 180 deg.

<u>Icing mixture to go on top of biscuits</u>
Beat 1 egg white till firm (white peaks)
Add icing sugar and mix well. Put aside for later use.

<u>Biscuit mixture</u>
Place 3 egg yolks, 2 egg whites, grated lemon peel, sugar and vanilla in bowl. Beat with electric mixer until it is pale in colour. Add flour and mix with wooden spoon. Place 1/3 of the mixture onto a floured board. Gently roll mixture into a 4 cm diameter and roll it to fit the length of the board.
Press down with hand and fingers to 1 1/2cm thickness
Cover with icing sugar and egg white mixture.
Sprinkle crushed peanuts on top and cut into 2cm wide pieces
Place on baking tray lined with baking paper and
place in 180 deg oven for 10 minutes.
Allow to cool on wire tray.

168

Biscotti cu Icing Sugar

INGREDIENTS
Makes 40 biscuits

- 6 eggs
- 1 cup of white sugar
- 125 gms of butter, softened
- 3 teaspoons of vanilla extract
- 1 lemon peel grated
- 530 grms of self raising flour (sifted)
- icing sugar to coat
- 200mls of vegetable oil

Heat oven to 180 degrees
Place eggs, grated lemon peel, sugar, vanilla, and oil in bowl.
Beat with electric mixer
Add flour and mix with wooden spoon.
Sprinkle icing sugar on board
Roll mixture into 10cm long pieces with a 2cms diameter.
Place on baking tray lined with baking paper.
Place in 180 deg oven for 13-15 minutes until brown on top

Cassata

Allow both ice creams to go soft
Place first layer of sponge cake into a 50 to 60 mm deep dish.
Sprinkle evenly with all 4 liquors. (not completely covered)
Sprinkle cherries, pineapple, apricots and almonds onto cake
As a second layer.
Spread a 12mm thick layer of soft vanilla ice cream over the lot.
Repeat second layer again with cake, liquor, and fruits and
finish off lastly with layer of soft chocolate ice cream
spread evenly over fruit.
Decorate top with vanilla ice cream and finish off with almonds.

Place in freezer for 24 hours.
The next day, once the ice cream has set, remove the
Cassata upside down from the dish, cut into 2 long pieces
and wrap in aluminum foil and place in freezer.

Cut into slices and serve cold.

INGREDIENTS
Makes 16 slices

- 500 mls Vanilla ice cream
- 500 mls Chocolate ice cream
- 50 gms glace cherries
- 1 1/2 rings of glace pineapple finely chopped.
- 4 dried apricots
- Sponge cake cut into 1 cm thick layers
- 25 gms of almond flakes
- Marsala liquor
- Strega liquor
- Midore liquor
- Cherry Brandy

INGREDIENTS
Serves 6 persons

PASTRY
- 1 egg
- 1 heaped tablespoon of softened butter
- 2 heaped tablespoons of caster sugar
- ½ cup of plain flour
- ½ cup of self raising flour

WHITE FILLING
- 2 cups of milk
- 2 heaped tablespoons of sugar
- 1 cinnamon stick
- Peel of one lemon
- 2 tablespoons of cornflour

ORANGE JELLY
- 2 cups of fresh squeezed orange juice
- 2 tablespoons of sugar (sugar is not needed if oranges are very sweet)
- 2 tablespoons of custard powder dissolved in small amount of water.

Jelly Tart di Zia Lisa

Heat oven to 180 degrees

Place both of the flours and sugar into a bowl. Add the soft butter using your fingers to mix it into the flour until the mixture resembles bread crumbs. Add the egg and mix thoroughly until the mixture combines. Place the mixture onto a board and knead until it is smooth. Wrap in gladwrap and let sit for about ½ and hour.

Prepare a 25cm pastry dish by rubbing some butter and dusting it with flour. Roll out the pastry with a rolling pin till it is approx 1cm in thickness. Place the pastry onto the prepared dish and bake in the oven for 15 - 20 mins or till the pastry is golden brown.

WHITE FILLING
In a saucepan add the milk, cinnamon, lemon peel and sugar. Heat the mixture till the milk is nearly boiling. Remove from the stove and strain into another saucepan of the same size. Return the mixture to the stove and add the cornflour which has been dissolved in a small amount of milk. Stir continuously till the mixture thickens. Remove from the stove and pour the mixture into the cooked pastry. Place in the fridge.

ORANGE JELLY FILLING
Place all ingredients into a saucepan and bring to the boil stirring continuously till the mixture thickens. Remove from the stove.

Take the tart from the fridge and pour the orange jelly mixture onto the tart by pouring the mixture on the back of a large spoon, so it spreads evenly over the tart. Place the tart into the fridge for at least 6 hours or overnight to set.

Crostolli

Mix flour, caster sugar, egg and Cinzano by hand with finger tips... keep mixing until combined and then knead until smooth. Cut mixture into 10cm sq pieces and 1cm s thick. Pass it through a pasta machine. Start on No 1, keep folding the dough sheet and increase the pasta machine setting to N3. Keep doing this until the pasta sheet is silky smooth.

Cut the thin sheets into 4 cm wide strips and cut a slot in the, middle, but not right to the ends.

Fold one end through the slot and stretch to make a sort of bow tie. Deep fry in hot oil until golden brown. Once golden brown remove from pan and drain excess oil by placing them on paper towels. Allow to cool.

Place on serving tray and sprinkle with icing sugar through a sieve.

INGREDIENTS
Makes 50 pieces

- 2 cups of plain flour
- 40 gms of lard
- 1 tablespoon of Caster sugar
- 1 egg
- ½ cup of Cinzano Bianco
- 1 tablespoon of icing sugar
- Vegetable oil for deep frying

Tiramisu

INGREDIENTS
Serves 8 persons

Crema di Zia Concetta :
- 4 cups of water
- 1 cinnamon stick roughly crushed
- 4 coffee beans
- Peel of 1 lemon
- 1 can condensed milk (reduced fat works just as well)
- 4 egg yolks

Tiramisu
- 1 batch of Italian cream both white and chocolate. (Still warm)
- 28 x 18 rectangle dish or pan
- 1 packet of saviordi biscuits
- 3/4 cup of espresso coffee (made in an Italian stove top peculator)
- Sugar to sweeten the coffee.
- 1 cup of milk
- 3 tablespoons of Galliano (more or less if that is what you prefer)

Keep a little extra coffee to make more soaking mixture, if needed.

Crema di Zia Concetta
(This is made in 3 parts. First the base is made then the white cream then the chocolate cream. Whisk to mix the ingredients to reduce any lumpiness that the cream may form.)

Place water, crushed cinnamon stick, coffee beans and lemon peel in a medium sized saucepan and bring to the boil.
Once the mixture has boiled strain into another medium sized saucepan and discard the peel, coffee beans and cinnamon stick.
If you find that there are bits of cinnamon in the mixture strain it through a bit of muslin. Add the condensed milk and stir till the condensed milk has dissolved. Once the mixture is tepid add the lightly beaten egg yolks to the mixture with a
whisk ensuring that the eggs are thoroughly mixed through.
Separate the mix in half into 2 medium sized saucepans.

Tiramisu:
Place the coffee, milk and liqueur into a shallow dish, stir to combine.
One by one soak the saviordi biscuits and place in the dish creating the first layer. Once you have done this spread the white Italian cream over the first layer.
Proceed soaking the remaining saviordi biscuits one by one and create another layer on top of the white one by gently pressing the biscuits into the white cream.
Place the chocolate cream on top of this final layer.
Place in the fridge to set.

Turdiddri

Place oil, wine and salt in a medium sized saucepan and bring to the boil for two minutes. Remove from stove and cool till tepid just until you can resist the heat with your hand.
Add flour to mixture and combine well.
Then turn out onto a lightly floured board/bench top.

Then make gnocchi. 2.5cm in length on average and 2cm in diameter. Make sure they are the same size otherwise they won't cook evenly.

Heat up oil in saucepan (enough to cover them) then deep fry on a stable medium heat in small batches until solid and golden brown.
Once cooked they will rise to the surface of the oil. Remove with a slotted spoon and place on absorbent paper.
Heat the honey on the stove till it starts to boil.
Add Turdiddri to the honey and toss to coat for about 2mins.
Remove with a slotted spoon and sprinkle with 100's @ 1000's.
Place in fridge and serve when cooled.

INGREDIENTS

. Two cups of red wine

. One cup of olive oil

. Heaped Tea spoon of salt

. Plain flour 1kg

. 1 cup of honey

. 100's & 1000's to sprinkle

Torrone

INGREDIENTS
Makes 40 pieces

- 400 Gms of roasted peanuts
- 2 tablespoons white sugar
- 3 tablespoons honey
- 100's & 1000's to sprinkle.

Lightly roast natural unsalted peanuts in the oven. Allow to cool and spread onto a chopping board. Using a rolling pin, crush the peanuts into medium small pieces. Place into a large deep frying pan and add the sugar and honey. Mix well.
Reduce heat to low and cook slowly, stir continuously for approximately 40 minutes. Make sure not to burn the peanuts. Once the peanuts are golden brown and cooked, spread the mixture onto a chopping board and shape into a rectangle, approximately 1 ½ cm thick. Sprinkle 100's & 1000's over and allow to cool.
Once they are cool to touch, cut into small bite size pieces and place in fridge to cool.
Once they are cool they are ready to serve.

Crema di Zia Concetta

INGREDIENTS
Makes 1 ½ litres

- 4 cups of water
- 1 cinnamon stick roughly crushed
- 4 coffee beans
- Peel of 1 lemon
- 1 can of condensed milk. reduced fat works just as well.
- 4 egg yolks

WHITE CREAM
- 2 heaped tablespoons of custard powder dissolved in a small amount of milk
- 2 tablespoons of Galliano
- ½ teaspoon of butter

CHOCOLATE CREAM
- 1/3 cup of cornflour dissolved in small amount of milk
- 125grams of good quality dark cooking chocolate broken into bits
- ½ teaspoon of butter
- 2 tablespoons of Galliano

This is made in 3 parts.
First the base is made then the white cream then the chocolate cream.
Use a whisk to mix the ingredients as it reduces any lumpiness the cream may form.

Place water, crushed cinnamon stick, coffee beans and lemon peel in a medium sized saucepan and bring to the boil.
Once the mixture has boiled strain into another medium sized saucepan and discard the peel, coffee beans and cinnamon stick.
(If there are bits of cinnamon in the mixture strain it through a bit of muslin).
Add the condensed milk and stir till the condensed milk has dissolved.
When the mixture is tepid add the lightly beaten egg yolks to the mixture with a whisk ensuring that the eggs are thoroughly mixed through.
Separate the mixture in half into 2 medium sized saucepans.

White Cream
Place one of the saucepans with half of the mixture on the stove on high heat.
Add the dissolved custard powder and stir the mixture constantly till it starts to boil and thicken. Remove from the stove and add the butter then the Galliano.
The cream is now ready.
To prevent it forming a skin on top place cling wrap directly on the cream and set aside.

Chocolate cream
Place the remaining saucepan containing the base mixture on to the stove with the dissolved cornflour and chocolate on high heat.
Stir constantly till the mixture boils and thickens.
Remove from the heat add the butter then the Galliano.
Cover with cling wrap to prevent a skin from forming on the top.
The cream is now ready to use to ice a cake, fill Cannoli or to make Tiramisu

Scavudatieddri.

INGREDIENTS
Makes approx 75

- 1 kg plain flour
- 1/2 cup oil
- 7gms yeast
- 1/2 teaspoon aniseed
- 2 3/4 cups of soda water
- 10 gms salt
- Extra 75 mls of water

Heat oven to 250 degrees. Dissolve yeast in soda water.
Place flour in bowl, make a well and add oil, salt, aniseed and yeast.
Mix by hand and knead in the bowl. Turn dough out onto a clean dry surface and keep kneading until it is smooth.
Cover with a table cloth and allow to sit for 5 min.
Cut into 5 smaller portions and keep kneading until silky smooth.
Roll dough by hand into a long thin tube (1.5 cm thick)
Cut the tube into 20cm long pieces and fold into circles, pressing ends together. Allow to sit for a couple of minutes
Bring to the boil a large pot of water and place 5 at a time into the boiling water. Remove from water as they start to rise slightly and place into bowl of cold water for approx 15 sec.
Drain and place on a baking tray lined with baking paper.
Place in the 250deg oven until golden brown. Approx 30min.
Once cooked, allow to cool on table cloth.

Panini, Pitta e` Pane

INGREDIENTS

Makes
40 panini,
5 pitti
14 small pane

- 7 Kg bakers flour
- 7 litres of water
- 70 grms of fresh yeast
- 1 heaped tablespoon salt.

This recipe is best done in a traditional wood fired oven and is included in our cook book more as a way of preserving this ancient traditional recipe. If you intend to try this recipe, it would be best to firstly make it a few times with someone who has done it before and of course has achieved reasonable results. Don't be disheartened, if it does not go to plan on your first couple of attempts... This does take a lot of practice and when it does work, the results are truly spectacular.

Start with lighting the wood in the oven and make sure that the final temperature is even all round and also between the bottom and top of the oven...
A 1 metre dia oven will use approximately 1 full wheelbarrow of wood. The flames will heat the top of the oven and then spread the hot coals evenly around the base to heat the bottom.
After 4 hours, most of the coals should have reduced to ash or very small bits. Remove all the ash / coals and clean the base of the oven with a damp rag mop. Allow the oven to sit for 5 minutes and check the temperature by sprinkling half a hand full of flour onto the base... If the flour burns quickly, pass the damp mop over the base a couple of times... Allow to sit again and test again.
When the flour browns slowly, the oven is ready for baking.

1 hour after lighting the wood fired oven, start with the dough. Sift all the flour into a large round plastic containers and add the salt, dissolved yeast and slowly keep adding water whilst continually mixing the dough by hand until all the flour is thoroughly mixed smooth and without lumps. Knead the dough with punching action, making sure you get down to the bottom and then also grab the dough from the bottom with both hands and stretch it by pulling upwards. Cover with thick cloth and allow to rest and rise. Repeat the previous kneading actions after the dough has risen to double its size and cover again. Repeat again for the 3rd time.
The dough is ready when it has risen and looks light and fluffy.

Preparing the dough for baking Panini and Pitta:
Grab a handful (40 gms) of dough and either cut it off with a knife or squeeze it off with your other hand.
Place it on a floured cloth (handkerchief size) and lightly use your fingers to tuck it into a ball, cover and allow to rest. Repeat this for all the dough to make panini and pitta. Cover the remaining dough in the container and leave for later on to make the pane.

Press down by hand, all the dough balls into a pizza shape and cover.. Allow to rest for 10 minutes. Flip the flatted round dough onto its other side and press the dough down till it is has about a 2cm thickness.

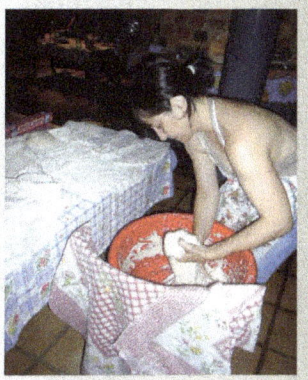
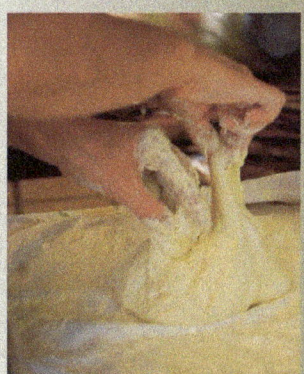

Baking the panini:

Use a 10 cm diameter metal tin to cut each small shape for the panini.
Place the panini directly into the oven with a timber paddle for cooking.
If the oven temperature is slightly too hot you can place the panini on metal trays...
Once all the panini are all cooked, the oven should be the correct temperature to bake the pitti.
Once you've make enough panini, the remaining flattened out dough will be used for pitta.
Remove the panini from the oven when they have risen and are golden brown.

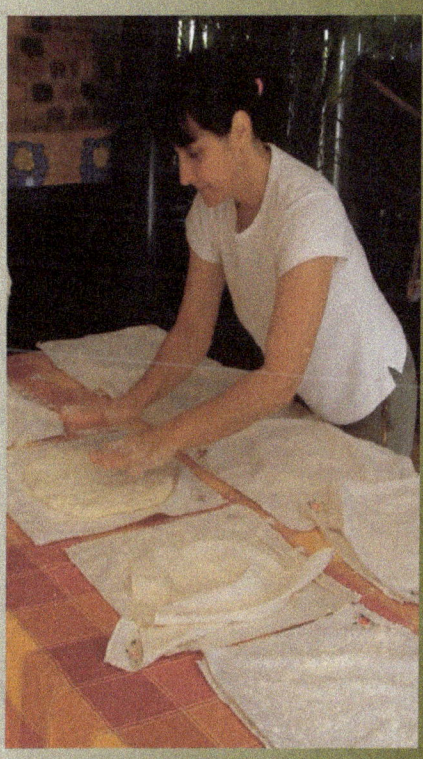

Panini, Pitta e` Pane

Baking the Pitta:

Lightly flour the paddle and place it beside the flattened dough and flip the dough onto the paddle. Use the tin to cut a hole in the middle which will make an extra panini. Slide the pitta dough from the paddle into the oven and repeat the process for the remaining pitti. Allow to rise and cook until golden brown. Check to make sure the bottoms are not burning, and put on trays if the base is starting to go slightly black. Remove the pitti when they are golden brown and light in weight. Repeat the baking process if you have an extra batch of pitti to bake.

During all the baking the top of the oven may have lost it's heat, so to do final baking of the pane, you will need to relight a small fire on the oven using only small twigs for the flame to reheat the top of the oven. When the flames have died down, remove the coals and clean the base with the damp mop ready for baking the Pane

Baking the Pane:

Whilst the oven is being reheated, grab a hand full (400 gms) of dough and either cut it off with a knife or squeeze it off with your other hand. Place it onto the same floured cloth and lightly roll into a cylinder and cover. Repeat for the remaining dough.
When the oven is ready, flip the pane onto the timber paddle and with a knife score 2 cuts along the length of the dough and slide into the oven. Repeat for the remaining dough. The pane should have all risen and browned after 30 minutes. Once brown, open the door to the oven and allow to cook for approximately another 30 minutes or until light in weight. Remove for the oven and allow to cool.
Once cooled off dust off excess flour off all the bread, place in plastic bags and freeze for future use.

184

LA RACOLTA
ZIO OTTORINO

A SHORT REST....
CONTEMPLATING
TOMORROW
WE MAKE
THE
WINE

Zia Aquilina

Making Wine

www.ingramcontent.com/pod-product-compliance
Lightning Source LLC
Chambersburg PA
CBHW061811290426
44110CB00026B/2851